BREATHING LESSONS

BREATHING LESSONS

poems by

SUSAN A. JEFTS

SHANTI ARTS PUBLISHING

BRUNSWICK, MAINE

Published by Shanti Arts Publishing

Designed by Shanti Arts Designs

Cover image: Tobias Tullius on unsplash.com

Shanti Arts LLC
193 Hillside Road
Brunswick, Maine 04011
shantiarts.com

Printed in the United States of America

ISBN: 978-1-962082-04-4 (softcover)

Library of Congress Control Number: 2023946666

*This book is in memory of my late parents,
Helen and Charlie Jefts.*

*For my father, who never stopped encouraging me as a
child to write and create and who imbued in me a deep love
and respect for all of the natural world. And for my mother,
whose strong organizational and editing skills I came to
truly value (and hopefully emulate) and who gradually
came to appreciate my unpredictable creative spirit.*

*This book is also for my dear friends and family who
have been so supportive of my writing over the years,
often accompanying me on hiking, paddling, and
travel adventures that inspired many of my poems.*

*The poems of this book are also for the forests,
mountains, lakes, and rivers, and their flow of
life, wisdom, and purity that are always inviting
us to come close, open our hearts, and listen.*

CONTENTS

ACKNOWLEDGMENTS

I wish to acknowledge the many poetry and writing teachers and mentors I have had over the years from whom I have learned so much. Many thanks to my first editor, April Ossmann, for her meticulous eye and ear, and ongoing encouragement with all aspects of my manuscript. To Arthur Sze, my teacher at Bread Loaf, who encouraged me to see poetry in ways I never had imagined. To the late Paul Pines, who fused jazz, art, Jungian psychology, and much more with poetry, making it more fun than I ever thought it could be. To Peggy Heller, an early mentor, who taught me about the power of poetry to awaken, enliven, and heal. And thank you to Christine Cote, the editor at Shanti Arts for her artful and thoughtful eye through all phases of the editing and book publishing process.

I wish to acknowledge and thank all my writer friends and the groups I've been part of in Saratoga Springs, the Adirondacks, and Middlebury, Vermont; all have given me invaluable feedback at one time or another on my poems, many of which are in this book.

I also wish to acknowledge the editors of the following publications where these poems previously appeared, sometimes in earlier versions.

A Slant of Light Anthology, Codhill Press: "Returning to Earth"

Addison County Independent: "One Gesture at a Time" and "Winter Solstice"

Best of Burlington Anthology 2017: "Blue Hour in the City" and "Night Flight"

Big City Lit, Hudson Headwaters Press: "Bardo Over the Hudson"

Birchsong II Anthology: "After the Lecture on Duende" and "Before Anything"

Blueline Literary Journal: "After the Lecture on Duende"

Blue Stone Review: "At Morikami Gardens"

Every Drop of Water: "April"

Fired Up: "The Tremor"

Mountain Troubadour: "Before Coffee" and "Returning to Earth"

Parnassus Literary Journal: "At Morikami Gardens"

Plant-Human Quarterly: "Before Anything" and "Even Though"

Poems in the Time of Covid, Small Pond Press: "Even Now"

Quiet Diamonds, 2021 Anthology, Orchard Street Press: "Arrival"

Quiet Diamonds, 2023 Anthology, Orchard Street Press: "The Juxtaposed Open Their Boundaries to One Another"

The Gardan Journal: "Tentatively"

Zig Zag Magazine: "Art in Springtime"

We live most life, whoever breathes most air.

—Elizabeth Barrett Browning

BLUE HOUR IN THE CITY

If we could measure
the light that is left,
that falls out of nowhere
we have been—we would
discover the place just
beyond the building spires
that make a point, like
sharpened graphite
on the sky as it moves
into night, but really,
it's the early part of
the blue hour—
that sacred time just
beyond day, just before
dusk that no one can
hold onto, and few
know how to truly enter.

EVEN NOW

Even now the lion sculpture by the river,
the one made of so many old metal washers,
shines as best it can in the subdued light.
The water rushing over the falls sounds
its deep chords, playing off the wind
in the maple and linden trees, and we
find the one spot of sun.

Even now, with this cool autumn falling,
we'll walk by the river, and we'll keep walking
past houses and fields, past statues standing
or fallen, through streets and over bridges,
below them the merging of so many colors—
red, brown, yellow and auburn—in cool
swirling waters. We'll make way
and keep making way, and send praise
to the day, to the towns that endure,
and to the lion that roars above the river
pulling particles of gold from the sun-flecked
air, from the autumn trees, sending them
out for the world, for the days ahead,
for the making way, for the roaring.

FAITH

Tonight I follow a shadowed path,
a narrow gauge of a place,
a half-dream walk
to darkness.

This gnarled door
opens slowly by itself
when I close my eyes
and this small lamp-light—
they share something.

The crickets' voices grow distant
like summer's fading breath,
and we too grow quiet in our sleep,

every year a lost footing
a slide toward nothing
and back again—
blossoms hanging on a vine
in autumn's half-born light.

RETURNING TO EARTH

It happened on a day I went to the woods,
a day I wore my blue scarf, savored an almond
muffin and shade-grown coffee. A day when
I thought about my conversation with Tay
at the café—images of rocks and roots
burst forth, and a bird in flight. It happened
on the day I finished my taxes.

It happened between one thing and another.
A book about the soul, a poem about things—
shoes and metal, tobacco smoke, and salt.
Many things conspired to tell me the whole
story, wrote Neruda, *not only those things*
that leap and climb, desire and survive.
A day teeming with things: the rust orange
on the chimes, the mailbox's blue. My book's
fibrous threads, the stone tablets in the park
—the way they sing, the way they stay still.
Now it seems I can't say enough about things.
How they connect me to a string in my body
that binds me to my soul. How every feeling
now is a stone or a book, tobacco smoke, or salt.

APRIL

Evening's earth scent
drifts through my window
holds me like the moment
just before rain, like
forsythia before it has
begun to bloom,
and the universe enters
my lungs, alveoli by alveoli.

In the distance, the river
runs fast as a night train,
and the halfmoon
hovers just over
the hill
like a suitor.

BREATHING

Mist gathers in the valley
rises to wreathe a cluster
of watchful pines.
I hear them breathe
through the window
we opened and then left open—
rain dripping off the eaves
onto the plank porch.
The sound I heard once
in a Japanese garden
between a bamboo grove
and a bridge, in me.

SAGUENAY

—L'Anse Saint Jean, Quebec

August's sun follows the ridgeline
down along the fjords, where
falcons fly from vertiginous
nests built on igneous rock
cloaked in balsam and fir.
Cliffs rise cathedral-like,
into blue topaz heavens
from black water below—
strange mix of lake, sea and river
—where a thousand feet down,
a thousand darknesses live,
where tiny bursts of life
pulse upward
with a luminescence
we cannot know,
while above the fjords,
falcons lean their wings
into the oblivious sky.

AFTER THE LECTURE ON DUENDE

—Bread Loaf, Vermont

If I were to write today about duende
I might not write from the gold-flecked
meadow or beneath the branches
of the apple trees at Frost's farm,
because duende comes from deep
in the earth, *and all that has*
dark sounds has duende, wrote Lorca.

I will write under the sky, though,
for who cannot know the sky,
or a butterfly's tinged wing
in August. I will write into the air,
hands cupped for receiving—
song of magpie, nectar's ooze,
goldenrod dust mid-air.
Soon the nights will cool,
the crickets will quiet,
and more apples will fall—
we can be assured of this.
How everything wants
to touch the earth
at least once.

A SINGLE CARNATION

The red carnation
on the stone table
on the lawn outside
the museum says wedding.
It says *together, alone.*

The Battenkill flows by,
higher this year than last.

We can see only as far
as the river bend;
one small shift
in the current
can alter its entire course.

Back on the lawn,
the wedding tent is empty.
Only a carnation remains.

AT MORIKAMI GARDENS

I am not a painter.
I do not speak Japanese.
But I feel these words in my bones,
hear their rat-a-tat in the bamboo
grove, feel their silk on my skin.
I hold to my lips a stone's mineral
taste, savor its softness against my palm.
I walk over winding pebbled paths,
to the *chashitsu*, onto
the wooden plank porch,
where I move inside
the wind—
and know at once, *mono-no-a-wabi*,
Japanese for "ahhhness."

PARADOX AT PUTNAM MARKET
DURING THE WINTER RAINS

I don't mind standing at the market waiting
for my turkey, avocado, and gruyere sandwich,
while I sample spiced jams, cheeses
from other countries, and inhale a thousand
aromas, even as torrential rains flood the streets,
and my relationship mudslides around me.
I feel the truth of what Auden said
(and Brueghel implied) about suffering—
how it happens when someone is opening
a window or, in this case, eating a sandwich—
though I don't know for sure I should call it suffering,
inevitable as it was from the start that it wouldn't last,
as different as we are. He would never see us
as a chapter or a poem needing to be written
in order to complete the book we are.
He would say life is the book we write as we
speak, fight, make up, repeat—crossed wires,
spilt milk, warts and all, but nothing truly ineffable.
Except this market's culinary creations; works of art
I will devour as if I were starving, art I taste
with every bud, so alive I almost begin to know myself.

BARDO OVER THE HUDSON

Words, born of vibrating air at
West 26th street. Words, dancing
patterns on the sidewalk, painting
themselves on purple pansies below
the Columbus statue in Central Park,
startling me out of any remaining winter.
Words, quivering outside Café Europa,
hovering between crème brûlée
and Carnegie Hall.

Words adorning the Hudson's wide
throat as my train rambles northward.
They flicker like newly born fireflies
unversed in the art of direction, or
rhythm, or sound. They are the ones
I want, these in-between words, lingering
in their bardo like spaces, sacred gaps
of which the mystics speak. Smoky mist
drifts low over the Hudson, between
Gotham and Lake Tear of the Clouds,
between life receiving and life giving.
Breath of being, breath of becoming.
Poetry.

A CELLO IN APRIL

The moan of a cello in April,
deep movement from under
the earth, dark sound beneath the city—
and outside a tree leans and listens
as people pass by the place
where the cello moans
slowly out of the depths,
as someone stops and pauses
and the cello breathes
more deeply as Earth holds
and releases, as the vibrato
hovers and reaches, rising
like a dark bird in flight,
low just over the city,
edged by the forest
that hums and sighs
at the rise of a cello in April,
and the dark bird in flight.

IF LIFE IS BUT A DREAM

Today was like the inside of white paper,
that kind of pure, and something in me
burned with a white heat so bright,
I understood the Lama from Tibet
who said plants are sentient,
and fire, water and air are too.

All afternoon I sat in air-conditioned rooms,
dreaming that my bicycle set me free
gliding under dappled tree light.
Perhaps tomorrow I will be free all day.
Walking home tonight, glass spheres
in a shop window reflect day's last light—
enough to make a small universe.
We wear the universe inside us,
said the Lama, *and we breathe*
it in and out all day.

When I stopped to pay attention to where my breathing was deep and settled, the truth began to emerge from the mist.

—Betsy Cañas Garmon

BEFORE COFFEE

Don't ask me to glue together
the shattered world,
or stop the February rain.
All I know—before thought,
before coffee, when words
are starlings, flitting
in and out of my mind—
is this space inside
that feels a little like God.
Nothing to fill, nothing to say,
just this pause,
this place,
before poetry.

GOAT DREAMS

Glancing in the mirror as I leave the house,
I glimpse something wild waiting to escape.
After working too long in this insubstantial winter
light, I kick back at the cafe with Eve and Tara.
Two glasses of wine, and I can't remember
what I was worried about an hour ago—
something about work and the stream
of ennui rising like an unwanted spring,
muddying otherwise solid earth. But now,
all my detritus may as well ring Saturn.
The night is sweet and cold and the moon
is new. A man plays guitar, sings of cities
and distant places, and I dream about
an old Greek island where people keep
bees, tend vines and goats on steep hillsides
with no fear of falling. I imagine meeting Eros
among olive, fig and cypress trees, and men
who wear the scent of soil and proffer good
sweet wine. Though I don't think the wine
would be for forgetting—it would be
for the trees and setting sun, a toast to say
thank you, after putting the goats to bed.

MICRO-MOVEMENTS

I see what the yoga teachers mean,
how each small movement is significant.
Near the brook's leafy edge of ferns
and moss, I move my cross-legged knee,
bringing myself a half inch closer
to ground and brook, my breath
a column of air between Earth
and sky. I am rooted like a fern,
but rocked, too, by the brook's
eddies that swirl around me—
back and forth, back and forth
in their spaces
not quite held, not quite free.

HERE, AGAIN

So much depends on the weather,
especially in April when the sky
becomes in seconds a thicket

of stones raining down, when grass
churns again with tiny creatures,
and the ground cannot be counted on

—soft and yielding in morning,
ice glazed pewter by afternoon.
The trees swell and contract,

swell and contract like lungs, with each
push of the bud. And the winged singing
from the waking Vermont woods and the wild

fruit trees in the fields, arranging your day
in a way your small thoughts
never could and you find yourself

standing morning after morning
on the steps of your front door,
looking out at the shifting sky and earth

while you waver between plunging
full bodied into it all, leaving behind
the dishes and scatter of paper,

or clasping your sweater around you
and returning, coffee mug in hand,
to the table that has kept you all these years

to what few others would find of consequence
but what sends you over and over through your
mind's waking field to its shimmering gold.

AFTER MEDITATION

Is this the narrow place,
the pause before
the expansion
—the place where resistance lies?
The way we fabricate soul,
the way we fall to depth.
Moonlight on a page
meets a tree's shadow
and when the wind
comes up, they dance.
I can't say I've ever
had this thought before.
I cannot say I've truly
learned to breathe.

GHOST POEMS

Sometimes I sense them
sitting just out of sight
like a ship around a point
or just off shore—ensconced
in fog. You feel their weighty
presence, maybe even see
their faint outline or a bit
of color seeping through.
You hear them listing gently
as the tide moves in
or out and, inevitably,
that unmistakable sound
of mast against metal,
like a bell or a chime
—a note awakened—
trying to work its way
into this world.

FIRST TUESDAY IN NOVEMBER

This morning, I step back from chaos,
leave my laptop and take myself to breakfast
at the Stone Café by the lake. I sit near
the corner window, breathe in fresh baked
bread and sip cinnamon swirled coffee,
while outside dry leaves pinwheel across the patio.
I could have easily gone with anger and angst—
a week of frustration, more turmoil coming
through every airwave—but I choose this instead.
In one sweep of my eyes over this Adirondack lake
I breathe in more than any liquid crystal screen
could ever hold, whose bytes and bits
could never conjure anything close to this
living display before me. Particles arranging
and rearranging into indigo rippled
water under russet threaded mountains—
at a pace I am sure I can keep up with.

THE NATURE OF QUIET

When quiet envelops me again
I will have turned off the news,
I will have walked away
from the computer, laid down
my pen. In my quiet,
I will hear each rain drop's
solo beat against the shingled roof.
They will not shout one over another,
they will not compete with the wind
to sing loudest, nor will I.
My quiet will be quiet too,
and my thoughts will have turned
away from the clamor and chaos
of this nation's days, to the stillness
of afternoon, just before
a single crow cries out
from the hushed field.
Then another
and another.

YOU AND I, AND THE RIVER

—Schuylerville, New York

I want to talk to the river,
as I traverse the towpath
that traces its bank.
I want to hear about its age
and unwieldy history,
its torrid colonial chapters
of war and surrender—
and its quiet companions
like us, rapt,
between bouts of rocks
and white water.
Like now,
between one struggle
and the next
where we can say *Here,*
lie down, rest a while, breathe—
the river will be at peace.
You can see it there
in the October sky,
as the trees' fiery reds
shimmer like gods
inside the water.

ON THE BLUFF AT MILITARY PARK, GETTYSBURG

I feel how war could happen here.
How the rolling hills, thick woods, and open fields would allow it.
I hear the wind's drumbeat in the cold March sun.

I see how the west wind pushes the long grasses down.
The wind strafes my hair, my skin, even the granite.
I feel how war could happen here.

People speak of the peace they feel when they come here.
I feel something, too.
I hear the wind's drumbeat in the cold March sun.

But I'm not sure I'd call it peace;
it's an uneasy presence.
I feel that war has happened here.

Perhaps it's what was here before the war,
some essence slowly working its way back.
I hear the drumbeat in the cold March sun.

Something seeping up through the cold
slowly thawing ground, to the brown-gold tips of grass.
I can feel how war has happened here,
and I hear the wind's drumbeat in the cold March sun.

THE TREMOR

Nothing fell that morning, no rain,
no mist, no snow, no color from
the January sky. No leaves from the trees.
But something was beginning—a tremor
from alleys and avenues, suburbs, projects,
and the furthest farms and forests. A tremor
made by the feet carrying the people, made
by the heartbeats of thousands, and thousands
more none thought would come, but they came
and made that vibration, pulled it up through
their soles, trembling their breath,
their cities, their nation.

Their rising voices thundered out their spoken,
written, and sung words over rooftops, steeples,
abandoned lots, factories, houses, and streets.
Thunder of the old, of families with babies, people
in wheelchairs, women, and more women, and men
who stood alongside. *I'm with her, and her, and her,*
read signs with arrows pointing to the crowd,
and *I'm with her,* next to an image
of a green and blue Earth.

This thunder defied gravity, coming from ground
to sound the sky, a soulful oneness rising like
the duende from thundering soles. The sun
shone through, brightening the city for a moment,

and held the thousands of bright voices joining millions all over the globe, holding all that day and night. Holding even now, sky resounding with Earth's tremors.

THE JUXTAPOSED OPEN THEIR BOUNDARIES
TO ONE ANOTHER

And so the rain
slides down the world
outside my window
slides down the music too
spare as gray mist sky
that earlier was mountains.
Spare as a single voice
sung over a few notes,
the one I hear on the radio
—*It's a Wonderful World,*
and now the one coming
from my own throat,
and the rain keeps sliding down.
I can touch it now
from the inside.

SOMETHING THERE IS

about a month, that is other
than a month or any wedge of time,
the way a window is not only
a thing that separates the inside
from the out. The way some things
are not stable, but change from
particle to wave and back,
as with hours and days,
as with the passing of someone
you knew a very long time,
from this realm to the next—
or, as my Native friend says,
just beyond the hill,
not so very far.

A sight I have seen
when the world we live in
borders, for a moment,
another world—
when it's not about time
at all, but more a curtain
breathing in the wind
that only you can see.

LAPLAND NIGHTS

The falling snow weaves
a gossamer veil
between worlds,
as if to offer each
a partial view of the other,
a movement toward truth.

Your face at the winter lake
was this kind of true.
So unexpectedly
we came upon
each other,
you had no time to prepare.
No groomed words, no charm—
only the wind in your breath,
and the tall pines
reflected in your eyes
snow lit and soft.

TENTATIVELY

These thoughts we send
in silence, as a fern sends
exploratory runners.
Cool nights when the
woodstove sputters and hums,
as winter ends and spring
has not yet come.
Nothing quite knows
what to do—the garden
lies brown and tangled,
awaiting new earthshine.
Sparrows dart back
and forth
in the dusky light
of not yet daffodils,
not yet brightly alive.

ART IN SPRINGTIME

When facts leave you,
when you've banished them
and their limited minds
and you walk through untamed air,
past extravagant magnolia,
chokeberry, forsythia
and jealous pines—
you make a place for art
and all things that enter us quietly,
like the color of stone, like age.
For what can come only
through pause and circumspect,
through attention so rapt, you hear
the throat's pulsing artery—
that certain highway to the heart.

A SIGHTING

Driving dusty Creek Road's
looping bend, where the old
farmhouse faces two directions—
I saw the palomino in a cast
of car headlights, moonlight,
and shadows. She was turning
into the locust grove
but not before glancing back.
It felt like a dream—mine
or someone else's. A horse
appearing out of the darkness,
a sighting of something
unexpected and complete,
and the turning away.

THE UNEARTHING

We fill the orchard with the noise
of our words, creaks of our steps.
Breathe in grape vine and apple,
air just past sweet.

Words emerge from the smallest places—
the honeycomb's gold-lit rooms,
bittersweet's fading red, dust of aster blue.
The small marble of sun lighting autumn.

They shoulder their way through Earth's
dark mixtures. Ride fingers of sunlight along
an outstretched hand, find nape of
sun-warmed neck, the skin around our mouths.

We relish their multiple syllables on our tongues,
their small bright nutrients, their still potent seed.

EVEN THOUGH

I like to stay until the sun sets
on the October fields, wheat grass
and milkweed shimmering
toward sundown. The great apple
tree in the center mandaled by
a fresh mown path. Everything else
a tall sea of golden-brown swaying
toward auburn, before fading to earth.
But now, this Vermont field couldn't be
more alive—every stem, stalk, and blade,
every stubborn oak leaf still clinging,
even though we are well into autumn,
even though it's almost dusk.

Somewhere, on another part of Earth
someone is waking to a bright orange sun;
whole countries are halfway to spring.
A wild lily—ivory, yellow, and tangerine—
is right now leaning over her hillside,
shimmering into morning.

ONE GESTURE AT A TIME

Parsnips on the counter, nutmeg in the jar,
sage leaf and lemon balm pressed against the window.
A mystic on the airwaves speaks of spirit and courage;
bringing ourselves to the world one gesture at a time.
We each have an imprint inside us—an encoding
in the soul that unfolds under the sky, finding
its way upon the earth.

Winter is now upon us. The darkening sun will bear
down, pause, shift, and send itself back across
the sky as it always has, and we will hold the growing
days like tiny seeds in the open curve of our palms.
We will give to them our breath, and the long steady
work of our hands.

IN MORNING

Before forward movement,
before engagement with
the world, spiraling energy
and thoughts move through
the house that spirit built,
that lanterns light from
inside, that birds sing to
at first light.

Movements echoing other
movements in notes
and filaments, signatures
of sound sent from other
realms, or siphoned
from the piano
that sits in silence
in the shadows
in its music.

AT HIGH ROCK MARKET

We taste heirloom tomatoes,
tarragon, thyme, and cheese
from goats near Himanee's farm,
where they sleep under apple
trees in afternoon. We taste
sun-warmed cantaloupe
juice running down our wrists,
sweet cream and mint scenting
our lips. Rivulets of dew run
over our skin, earth's fruits
lingering on our tongues,
making slower our walking,
making longer our sighs,
making summer stay on—
past August, past touching,
past tasting,
—it stays.

ARRIVAL

When it happens, it just happens. It's the long night
unfolding into morning. It's the quick of a thing
gelling in mid-air. The slightest strand of wind lit
grass. There might be music, there might not.
It might be after many days of work

or while driving into the dark mountains. It might be
at the end of a long month, or a longer winter,
but there will be a shift—a relaxation in the body—
and a message that comes through and rises above
the throat. There will be a hundred forms of light

that arrive just for you, like an invitation. And you will know—
you are welcome here. That you belong.

Not just beautiful, though—the stars are like the trees in the forest, alive and breathing. And they're watching me.

—Haruki Murakami

TEACHINGS FROM THE BOG

—Norton Island, Maine

What is this circuitous, meandering route?
This muddling mass, this peat thickened soup—
this underground world of the bog.
The mire and muck, the layering and decomposing
the leaping from rock to rock. The quaking and gurgling,
sometimes sinking, grasping with both our hands.
Feeling and plumbing the roots on down to the darkest
underground, and pulling them up with the dirt
still on them till they make a popping sound.
We're steeped in earth, in bedrock and sediment,
in liquid pools of tannin flecks and granite specks
luring like fools' gold. We dodge hummocks
and hillocks, fall on our buttocks, and pick our
sodden selves up again. Oh the sphagnum,
the slime, the wet woolen rocks, but how they all
shine in the sun. We forage and festoon, finally
clambering on out of the fen—in the gray dawn,
the noon time, the pre-blue of evening, and now
the dark blue night. Desire's prescript, pleasure's
postscript. The first write and the last.
The deep cosmic moan of creating—
the bog loving, mud loving swoon.

PROKOFIEV, IN SUMMER

Allegro, Maestoso, Andante.
Each piece rains down—
the quick and furious,
the slow and dignified.
The unexpected sudden stop.
Morning emerges from
mist. Afternoon can't
escape evening's
blue sleeve.
Trees nod and whisper
between movements.

Yes, I remember you on such a night—
defiant, reverent, sublime
all at once. The song thrush
always calling from the highest branch—
our eyes floating upward in unison.

READING THE ANCIENTS ON A 21ST-CENTURY NIGHT

Is it a holy longing I feel?
Reading and re-reading till the words
become a wave of sound, an unearthed
song set free to find me here a thousand
years later, in my apartment up
near the treetops, braving
the crisscrossed city air abuzz
with radio waves and microwaves,
steel guitar and bass drifting up
from town over Oak and Linden trees.
But here, on this August night,
the sounds of the Upanishads, Li Po,
Kabir, and Hafiz—and the serenading
crickets outside my window—
are the ones that strum
my soul, like a banjo.

BEFORE ANYTHING

. . . is air and the smallest
stirring—leaf against leaf,
an insect or two teetering
on a grass blade. The dawn pushing
through to find us on a July day,
just after waking, just past sleep.

The vast green blur begins to differentiate
into many greens: willow and juniper,
olive green and sage. Peat moss
and fern and all their intimate relations,
and somewhere in the shadows,
the black green of decay.

And just across the river—apple orchard green.
Nascent fruits that will grow, transform in shape,
hue into harvest. It could take a lifetime to name
every green and what it can do. Even here,
in this moment of just born light,
we can breathe so much.

TO SWIM DEEP

All that is beautiful
that slips away—
a December night
that before was November
and September, and before that,
July when days were blue silver
waves we swam through.
Droplets alighted our skin,
grass became silk to our feet
under white birches—
day after day went on like that.
Now, this cold winter night
drift us into whiteness
and so we go into soft lit houses
with our books and our work,
and our voices that know
this is the time to dive deep
into questions put aside too long.
To go deep into this blue light,
the winter hours plunging
to where we might find
each other's shore,
you and I.

GEMS ALONG THE HUDSON

This river's northern reaches
could almost be Alaska or the Yukon.
The fast narrow channel snaking
the center, squeezed by ice
encroaching from either side,
cold as death. Mountains in the
distance, mountains close up.
Despite eighteen-degree air
the sun has just passed midwinter,
leaning us closer to spring.
I trace markings in the snow—
diamond mudras like the ones
I learned to make with my hands,
like the gleaming stones I found
last summer along the river's
edge, held a moment before
letting them go. I take one full
breath and turn toward the sun.

THE RISING

—Nantucket, Massachusetts

Last night at Siasconset,
fog dropped over the beach
like a cloak left by a passer by.
Everything—shore signs,
the pathway back—obscured
by the dense rolling gray,
and then came obsidian black.
This morning, steam rises slowly
off rain-soaked cobblestone.
Outside the church on Orange Street,
a balm of cello and piano reaches me
through stained glass windows.
I don't know whether chance,
instinct, or synchronicity
brought me here, but I begin
to sense a divine gathering
of earth, sky and ocean.
Here, where last night's mist
lingers among quotidian mysteries.

WAITING GROUND

How the geese arced wide
over the river, lowering
their wings to just the place
they wanted to be. How,
in midflight, the whole
of their bodies spoke through
the gliding heat of their wings.
It is no small thing to listen
to your beating heart—not
just the pulse but the blood
rushing—and follow it down
to the thousand ripples.
To the waiting ground.
Oh, what we carry and are carried by.

SOMETIMES IT HAPPENS THIS WAY

As on a September morning,
after paying some bills and making
coffee, after the sun had been up
a while. In that awake, but still,
place after breakfast and before
work, whatever work might be
that day. It was between one thought
and another, behind a cloud just over
the horizon, when I felt the world
surround me, but not close in.
The world backed away
and there it was like the poet
in the mountains said
—*coming over the horizon*—
a line of words, a feeling really,
a sensation cascading
so fast I couldn't catch it.
No time, even, to breathe.

So this is not quite it, and these words
only remnants of what passed through
from the near and far mystery—
something that wanted to be known,
if only briefly, before soaring back
over the fields, over the mountains,
to where invisible things are born.

NIGHT FLIGHT

When I look for wisdom tonight
I find aphorism in the mountain's
white ridge, shining in moonlight
like a possible future I could have faith in.
I sense more in places I can't quite see
where the mountain meets the valley,
where perhaps a rift has formed
holding onto night longer than
the rest of the vale. I hear
the night owl's gasp on her flight
through the black and ash pattern
of the forest, under the moon's
broken light threading its way
to an open field. All of it cast
blue as a Chagall—the field
rising like a flying carpet,
candles floating in the heavens,
drifting down to the river
of sacred swirling myth
flowing from the fertile valley,
the mountain perched like a chapel.

MOVING THROUGH NOVEMBER

I try to see what I can, hold close the light
as the light is, as if swimming through mist,
as it makes its diminishing way toward Solstice.

I make my way too, don a hat
and a jewel or two, make an occasion
of going across town or country, oceans even.

We ring a bell for thanksgiving, a psalm
for darkening days, paradox for comfort—
May the darkness be as light to you.
Everything holds a mystery.

Even our cells everyday are new,
as are we, opening and breathing
whatever light comes.

WINTER SOLSTICE

—Merck Forest, Vermont

The dry rustle of leaves
is what I remember,
and the lateness of the hour—
moon yet to appear.
Something ending,
something about to begin.
Wren makes a different sound than owl,
makes a different sound than snow
falling not quite silently
over December woods—
passion falling to darkness,
the loneliness of a body leaving,
as Earth turns imperceptibly
toward her spring.

THERE LIVES A JOY

There lives a joy in the body
and a body around that joy
that forgets from time to time
it was born when the body was born
to move through both the light and dark.

It came to dance, this joy; it says
to the body, *Come on, turn up
the music. Come dance until you can't.*
Dance despite winter, despots, greed,
and cowardice, and losses you never imagined.

It is for all of this that joy was born
into the body, reminding us to dance
in our light, in dark that forgets us,
even as it swallows us whole as Jonah.

But the joy—it always sees,
shining from inside the body.
And in the end it never forgets.
It was there when we were born,
there in our first breath.

UNDER THE BELFRY TOWER

If not the full moon waxing,
then the crescent arriving. If not
this week, then last. The moon
slipping slowly into the belfry tower,
while we watch from shadows
on the Green. It was June or July
—just past fireflies.

If not this year, then next. If not
our turn, someone else's—
but we decide it's ours. This town,
instead of another; these mountains,
not some far away. *This* arrangement
of atoms under a summer sky,
in the year of the Rabbit, between
Gemini and Cancer in the age
of Aquarius. The whole sky
is slowly shifting, astronomers say.
Great Bear might not be Great
Bear tomorrow. Orion might
loosen his belt and fly.

IF, IN THIS SPRINGTIME

If we could all be winged for a day
if we could call up our greenly spirits
our unfolding, our unfurling, our wings
like leaves, our leaves like wings—
think what we could do

for a day, then another, however long
they last, however far they go. Take us
to the unrowed river, the untilled soil,
the unsung songs, and take us back

to what was purest sound—
not voice, not music, but sounds
the world made sitting alongside itself,
drifting in its liquid pool

turning, vibrating ever gently
to the hum that made it
the universe hum that led
to the smallest quiver of air

the smallest leafy whorl, the first
flutter of what made the wing,
the greenly leaf. Made us.

SUSAN JEFTS returned in 2021 to the southern Adirondacks to build a home on family forest land overlooking Lake George, after spending several years in Middlebury, Vermont, and Saratoga Springs, New York. She leads groups using poetry to explore what we find meaningful and sacred in our lives and to deepen our felt connections to the vital world of forests, mountains, and water bodies. She offers these experiences in New York as well as Vermont, where she still spends time. In addition to writing, she works as a manuscript editor, facilitator of writing workshops, and poetry columnist. Her work has been published in many anthologies and journals including *A Slant of Light, Birchsong II, Quiet Diamonds, Poems in the Time of Covid, Plant-Human Quarterly, BlueStone Review, Blue Line Literary Magazine, Parnassus, Big City Lit, Best of Burlington Writers, The Gardan Journal, Zig Zag Magazine,* and *Fired Up,* among others. For more information, please visit Susan's website: SusanJefts.com.

Printed in the USA
CPSIA information can be obtained
at www.ICGtesting.com
LVHW041219060424
776609LV00008B/433

9 781962 082044